HAL•LEONARD
BLUES PLAY-ALONG
Book & CD for B♭, E♭, Bass Clef and C instruments

VOLUME 12

Jimmy Reed

PLAY 8 SONGS WITH A PROFESSIONAL BAND

HOW TO USE THE CD:

Each song has <u>two</u> tracks:

1) Full Stereo Mix

All recorded instruments are present on this track.

2) Split Track

Piano and **Bass** parts can be removed
by turning down the volume on the LEFT channel.

Guitar and **Harmonica** parts can be removed
by turning down the volume on the RIGHT channel.

Cover photo © Jan Persson/CTSIMAGES

ISBN 978-1-4234-9647-2

HAL•LEONARD®
CORPORATION
7777 W. BLUEMOUND RD. P.O. BOX 13819 MILWAUKEE, WI 53213

Visit Hal Leonard Online at
www.halleonard.com

Jimmy Reed

BOOK

CD

TITLE	CD Track Number Full Stereo Mix	CD Track Number Split Track
Ain't That Lovin' You Baby	1	9
Baby, What You Want Me to Do	2	10
Big Boss Man	3	11
Bright Lights, Big City	4	12
Going to New York	5	13
Honest I Do	6	14
You Don't Have to Go	7	15
You Got Me Dizzy	8	16

Ain't That Lovin' You Baby

Words and Music by
Jimmy Reed

Additional Lyrics

2. Let me tell you, baby,
   Don't sound like it's true.
   They could drop me in the ocean,
   I'd swim to the bank and
   Crawl home to you.

3. They may kill me, baby,
   Bury me just like they do.
   My body might lie,
   But my spirit gonna rise and
   Come home to you.

Baby, What You Want Me to Do

Words and Music by
Jimmy Reed

BA - BY, WHY YOU WAN - NA LET GO? _____ 2. GO - IN'

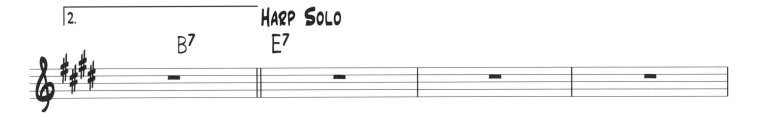

HARP SOLO

To Coda

D.S. AL CODA
(TAKE 2ND ENDING)

Coda

3. YOU GOT ME

(GUITAR)

ADDITIONAL LYRICS

2. Goin' up, goin' down.
   Goin' up, down, down, up any way you wanna, let it roll.
   Yeah, yeah, yeah.
   You got me doin' what you want me,
   Baby, why you wanna let go?

3. You got me peepin', you got me hidin',
   You got me peep, hide, hide, peep any way you wanna, let it roll.
   Yeah, yeah, yeah.
   You got me doin' what you want me,
   Baby, why you wanna let go?

Big Boss Man

Words and Music by
Al Smith and Luther Dixon

Additional Lyrics

2. Well, I'm gonna get me a boss man,
   One gonna treat me right.
   Work hard in the daytime,
   Rest easy at night.
   Big boss man,
   Can't you hear me when I call?
   Well, you ain't so big,
   You just tall, that's all.

CD TRACK

4 Full Stereo Mix

12 Split Mix

C Version

Bright Lights, Big City

Words and Music by
Jimmy Reed

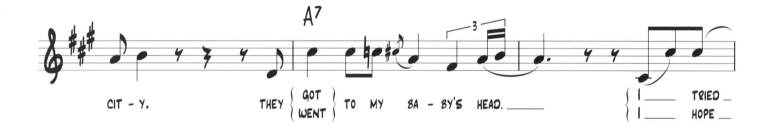

NEED MY HELP SOME - DAY.___ OH,___ YES AL - RIGHT.___ A PRET - TY

BA - BY,___ YOU'RE GON - NA NEED MY HELP __ SOME - DAY.___ YOU'RE GON - NA

WISH YOU HAD A LIS - TENED TO SOME OF THOSE THINGS I SAID.___

Solo

3

3. A GO ___

Verse

'HEAD ___ PRET - TY BA - BY,___ A HON - EY, KNOCK A YOUR - SELF OUT.___

OH,___ GO 'HEAD A PRET - TY BA - BY,___ A

HON - EY, KNOCK __ YOUR - SELF OUT.___ I ___ STILL ___ LOVE YOU BA - BY 'CAUSE YOU

D.S. al Fine

DON'T KNOW WHAT IT'S ALL A - BOUT.___ 4. BRIGHT

Going to New York

Words and Music by
Jimmy Reed and Mary Reed

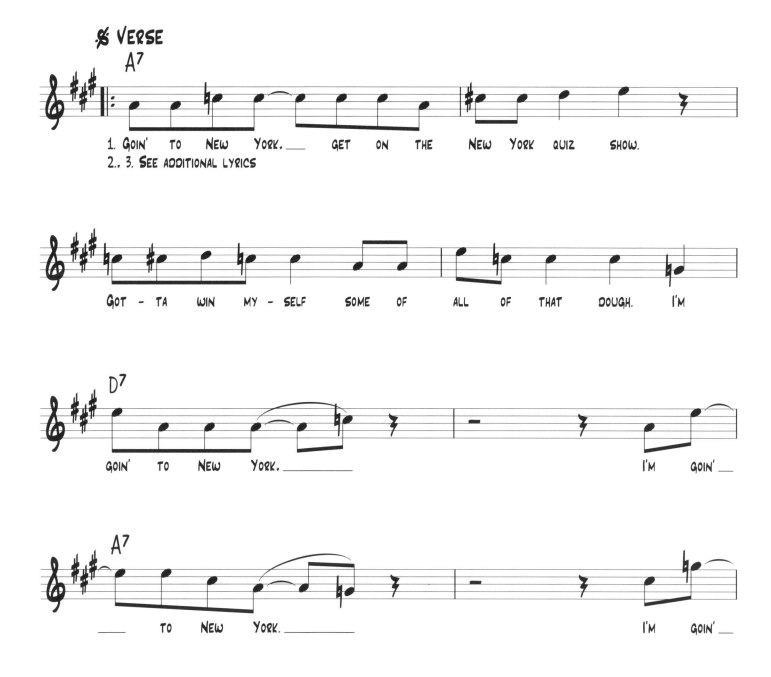

Intro-Solo
Moderate Shuffle ♩ = 96

% VERSE

1. Goin' to New York, ___ get on the New York quiz show.
2., 3. See additional lyrics

Got-ta win my-self some of all of that dough. I'm

goin' to New York. _____ I'm goin' _____

to New York. _____ I'm goin'

ADDITIONAL LYRICS

2. I've been down south, you know, I've been out east.
   I've been out west, but I'm not gonna rest 'til I
   Get to New York, I'm goin' to New York.
   I'm goin' to New York, I'm goin' if I have to walk.

3. I've been here, you know, I've been there.
   Honey, I've been some of everywhere, but I'm
   Goin' to New York, I'm goin' to New York.
   I'm goin' to New York, I'm goin' if I have to walk.

BRIDGE

Please tell me you love _____ me.

Stop driv - in' me mad. _____

You the sweet - est lit - tle wom - an

D.S. al Coda

that I ev - er had. _____

Coda   **OUTRO-SOLO**

(HARP)

Repeat and Fade

ADDITIONAL LYRICS

2. I told you I love you,
   Stop drivin' me mad.
   When I woke up this morning,
   I never felt so bad.

You Don't Have to Go

Words and Music by
Jimmy Reed

2. Well, I give you all my mon-ey then you go down-town. And you get back in the eve-ning told me walked down-town. Oh, ba - by, you don't have to go. ____ I'm gon-na pack up dar - lin', down the road I'll go. ____

3. Oh, ba - by, hon-ey what's wrong with you? ____ Oh, ba - by, hon-ey what's wrong with you? ____ Well, you don't treat me dar - lin', like you used to do. ____

STRAIGHT 8THS

YEAH, YOU GOT ME DIZ - ZY, AND I

CAN'T E - VEN SEE MY WAY. _____

HARP SOLOS

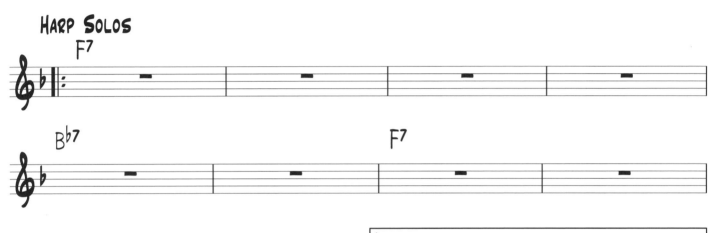

ADDITIONAL LYRICS

2. LET ME TELL YOU, BABE, WHAT I SAY IS TRUE.
   I AIN'T NEVER, NEVER LOVED NOBODY IN THE WAY THAT I LOVE YOU, NO,
   YOU GOT ME DIZZY,
   WHOA, YOU GOT ME DIZZY.
   YEAH, YOU GOT ME DIZZY
   AND I CAN'T EVEN SEE MY WAY.

3. WAIT A MINUTE, BABE, DON'T YOU BIP OR BOP.
   YOU DONE MADE ME LOVE YOU, BABY, AND I SWEAR I JUST CAN'T STOP,
   'CAUSE YOU GOT ME DIZZY,
   WHOA, YOU GOT ME DIZZY.
   YEAH, YOU GOT ME DIZZY
   AND I CAN'T EVEN SEE MY WAY.

Ain't That Lovin' You Baby

Words and Music by
Jimmy Reed

Additional Lyrics

2. Let me tell you, baby,
   Don't sound like it's true.
   They could drop me in the ocean,
   I'd swim to the bank and
   Crawl home to you.

3. They may kill me, baby,
   Bury me just like they do.
   My body might lie,
   But my spirit gonna rise and
   Come home to you.

Baby, What You Want Me to Do

Words and Music by
Jimmy Reed

INTRO
MEDIUM SHUFFLE ♩ = 96

1. You got me

※ VERSE

RUN - NIN', YOU GOT ME HID - IN', YOU GOT ME

2., 3. See additional lyrics

RUN, HIDE, HIDE, RUN AN - Y WAY YOU WAN - NA, LET IT

ROLL. YEAH, YEAH, YEAH. _____

YOU GOT ME DO - IN' WHAT YOU WANT ME.

F#7

1.

C#7

BA - BY, WHY YOU WAN - NA LET GO? _____

2. GO - IN'

2.

HARP SOLO

C#7   F#7

B7

F#7

TO CODA

C#7

F#7

D.S. AL CODA
(TAKE 2ND ENDING)

CODA

C#7

3. YOU GOT ME

(GUITAR)

ADDITIONAL LYRICS

2. GOIN' UP, GOIN' DOWN.
   GOIN' UP, DOWN, DOWN, UP ANY WAY YOU WANNA, LET IT ROLL.
   YEAH, YEAH, YEAH.
   YOU GOT ME DOIN' WHAT YOU WANT ME.
   BABY, WHY YOU WANNA LET GO?

3. YOU GOT ME PEEPIN', YOU GOT ME HIDIN',
   YOU GOT ME PEEP, HIDE, HIDE, PEEP ANY WAY YOU WANNA, LET IT ROLL.
   YEAH, YEAH, YEAH.
   YOU GOT ME DOIN' WHAT YOU WANT ME,
   BABY, WHY YOU WANNA LET GO?

Big Boss Man

Words and Music by
Al Smith and Luther Dixon

ADDITIONAL LYRICS

2. WELL, I'M GONNA GET ME A BOSS MAN,
   ONE GONNA TREAT ME RIGHT.
   WORK HARD IN THE DAYTIME,
   REST EASY AT NIGHT.
   BIG BOSS MAN,
   CAN'T YOU HEAR ME WHEN I CALL?
   WELL, YOU AIN'T SO BIG,
   YOU JUST TALL, THAT'S ALL.

BRIGHT LIGHTS, BIG CITY

Words and Music by
Jimmy Reed

1. Bright ___ Lights, Big Cit - y, They

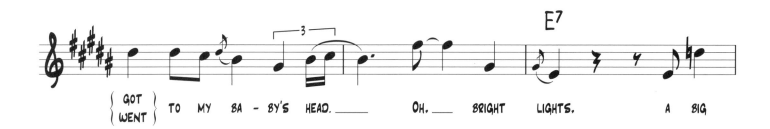

{ Got / Went } To My Ba - by's Head. ___ Oh, ___ Bright Lights, A Big

Cit - y, They { Got / Went } To My Ba - by's Head. ___ { I ___ Tried ___ / I ___ Hope ___ }

___ To Tell The Wom - an, But She Don't Be - lieve A Word I Said. ___
___ You Re - mem - ber A Some Of Those Things I Said. ___

VERSE

Fine (Fade last 2 bars)

2. Go ___ Light, Pret - ty Ba - by, ___ A

NEED MY HELP SOME-DAY. ___ OH, ___ YES AL - RIGHT, A PRET-TY

BA - BY, ___ YOU'RE GON - NA NEED MY HELP _ SOME-DAY. ___ YOU'RE GON - NA

WISH YOU HAD A LIS-TENED TO SOME OF THOSE THINGS I SAID. ___

SOLO

3

3. A GO ___

VERSE

'HEAD _____ PRET-TY BA-BY, ___ A HON-EY, KNOCK A YOUR - SELF OUT. __

OH, ___ GO 'HEAD A PRET-TY BA - BY, ___ A

HON-EY, KNOCK _ YOUR - SELF OUT. ___ I ___ STILL ___ LOVE YOU BA - BY 'CAUSE YOU

D.S. AL FINE

DON'T KNOW WHAT IT'S ALL A - BOUT. ___ 4. BRIGHT

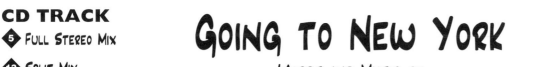

Going to New York

Words and Music by
Jimmy Reed and Mary Reed

1. Goin' to New York, __ get on the New York quiz show.
2., 3. See additional lyrics

Got-ta win my-self some of all of that dough. I'm

goin' to New York. __ I'm goin' __

__ to New York. __ I'm goin' __

Additional Lyrics

2. I've been down south, you know, I've been out east.
   I've been out west, but I'm not gonna rest 'til I
   Get to New York, I'm goin' to New York.
   I'm goin' to New York, I'm goin' if I have to walk.

3. I've been here, you know, I've been there.
   Honey, I've been some of everywhere, but I'm
   Goin' to New York, I'm goin' to New York.
   I'm goin' to New York, I'm goin' if I have to walk.

Honest I Do

Words and Music by
Jimmy Reed and Ewart G. Abner, Jr.

Intro-Solo
Slow Shuffle ♩ = 66

(HARP)

VERSE

1. Don't you know that I love _____ you,
2. See additional lyrics

HON - EST I DO.

I'D NEV - ER PLACE _____

NO ONE _____ A - BOVE YOU.

To Coda

BRIDGE
E7

Please tell me you love _____ me,

F#7

Stop driv-in' me mad. _____

You the sweet-est lit-tle wom — an

D.S. al Coda

B

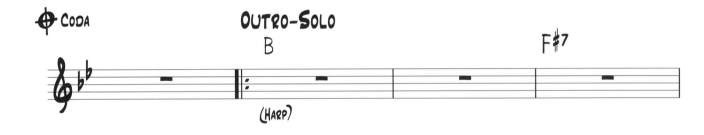

That I ev-er had. _____

⊕ Coda   OUTRO-SOLO
B   F#7

(Harp)

B   Repeat and Fade

Additional Lyrics

2. I told you I love you,
   Stop drivin' me mad.
   When I woke up this morning,
   I never felt so bad.

You Don't Have to Go

Words and Music by
Jimmy Reed

CD TRACK
7 Full Stereo Mix
15 Split Mix

Bb Version

INTRO
MEDIUM SLOW SHUFFLE ♩ = 84

(HARP)

VERSE

1. OH,

BA - BY, YOU DON'T HAVE TO GO. _____

OH, BA - BY, YOU DON'T HAVE TO GO. _____

_____ I'M GON-NA PACK UP DAR - LIN',

DOWN THE ROAD I'LL GO. _____

HARP SOLO

Yeah, you got me diz - zy, and I can't e - ven see my way. _____

Harp Solos

Additional Lyrics

2. Let me tell you, babe, what I say is true.
I ain't never, never loved nobody in the way that I love you, no.
You got me dizzy,
Whoa, you got me dizzy.
Yeah, you got me dizzy
And I can't even see my way.

3. Wait a minute, babe, don't you bip or bop.
You done made me love you, baby, and I swear I just can't stop.
'Cause you got me dizzy,
Whoa, you got me dizzy.
Yeah, you got me dizzy
And I can't even see my way.

Additional Lyrics

2. Let me tell you, baby,
   Don't sound like it's true.
   They could drop me in the ocean,
   I'd swim to the bank and
   Crawl home to you.

3. They may kill me, baby,
   Bury me just like they do.
   My body might lie,
   But my spirit gonna rise and
   Come home to you.

37

CD TRACK

◆2 Full Stereo Mix

◆10 Split Mix

Eb Version

Baby, What You Want Me to Do

Words and Music by
Jimmy Reed

INTRO
MEDIUM SHUFFLE ♩ = 96

1. You got me

.%. VERSE

RUN - NIN', YOU GOT ME HID - IN', YOU GOT ME
2., 3. See additional lyrics

RUN, HIDE, HIDE, RUN AN - Y WAY YOU WAN - NA, LET IT

ROLL. YEAH, YEAH, YEAH.

YOU GOT ME DO - IN' WHAT YOU WANT ME.

BA - BY, WHY YOU WAN - NA LET GO? _____

2. GO - IN'

HARP SOLO

To Coda

D.S. AL CODA
(TAKE 2ND ENDING)

CODA

3. YOU GOT ME

(GUITAR)

ADDITIONAL LYRICS

2. GOIN' UP, GOIN' DOWN,
   GOIN' UP, DOWN, DOWN, UP ANY WAY YOU WANNA, LET IT ROLL.
   YEAH, YEAH, YEAH.
   YOU GOT ME DOIN' WHAT YOU WANT ME,
   BABY, WHY YOU WANNA LET GO?

3. YOU GOT ME PEEPIN', YOU GOT ME HIDIN',
   YOU GOT ME PEEP, HIDE, HIDE, PEEP ANY WAY YOU WANNA, LET IT ROLL.
   YEAH, YEAH, YEAH.
   YOU GOT ME DOIN' WHAT YOU WANT ME,
   BABY, WHY YOU WANNA LET GO?

Eb Version

Big Boss Man

Words and Music by
Al Smith and Luther Dixon

ADDITIONAL LYRICS

2. Well, I'm gonna get me a boss man,
One gonna treat me right.
Work hard in the daytime,
Rest easy at night.
Big boss man.
Can't you hear me when I call?
Well, you ain't so big,
You just tall, that's all.

Going to New York

Words and Music by
Jimmy Reed and Mary Reed

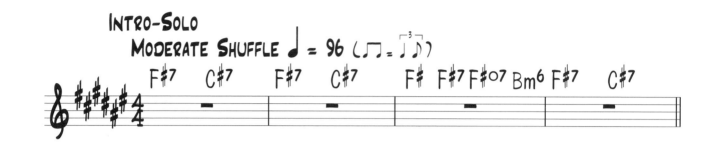

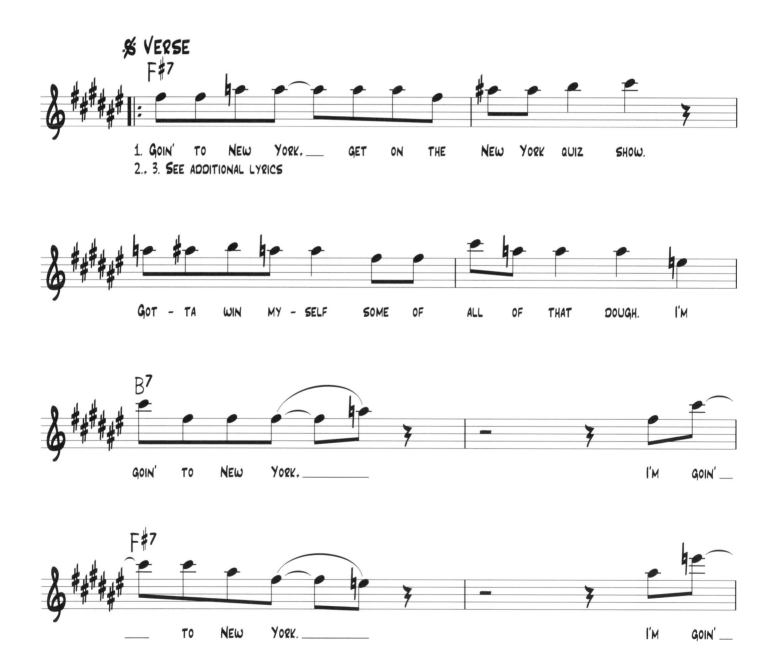

1. Goin' to New York,___ get on the New York quiz show.
2., 3. See additional lyrics

Got-ta win my-self some of all of that dough. I'm

goin' to New York._____ I'm goin'___

___ to New York._____ I'm goin'___

Harp/Guitar Solos

TO NEW YORK, I'M GOIN' IF I HAVE TO

WALK.

1.

2. I'VE

D.S. AL CODA
(TAKE 2ND ENDING)

CODA

w/ FILL

ADDITIONAL LYRICS

2. I'VE BEEN DOWN SOUTH, YOU KNOW, I'VE BEEN OUT EAST.
   I'VE BEEN OUT WEST, BUT I'M NOT GONNA REST 'TIL I
   GET TO NEW YORK. I'M GOIN' TO NEW YORK.
   I'M GOIN' TO NEW YORK, I'M GOIN' IF I HAVE TO WALK.

3. I'VE BEEN HERE, YOU KNOW, I'VE BEEN THERE.
   HONEY, I'VE BEEN SOME OF EVERYWHERE, BUT I'M
   GOIN' TO NEW YORK, I'M GOIN' TO NEW YORK.
   I'M GOIN' TO NEW YORK, I'M GOIN' IF I HAVE TO WALK.

Honest I Do

Words and Music by
Jimmy Reed and Ewart G. Abner, Jr.

INTRO-SOLO
SLOW SHUFFLE ♩ = 66

(HARP)

VERSE

1. Don't you know that I love _____ you.
2. See additional lyrics

HON - EST I DO. _____

I'D NEV - ER PLACE _____

NO ONE _____ A - BOVE YOU.

TO CODA

Additional Lyrics

2. I told you I love you.
Stop drivin' me mad.
When I woke up this morning,
I never felt so bad.

A⁷

YEAH, YOU GOT ME DIZ - ZY, AND I

G⁷

To Coda ⊕ D   G⁷   D   A⁷

CAN'T E - VEN SEE MY WAY. _____

HARP SOLOS

D⁷

G⁷   D⁷

A⁷   G⁷   ⌐1.⌐ D   A⁷

⌐2.⌐
D   G⁷   D   A⁷   D.S. AL CODA   ⊕ CODA   D N.C.   D⁷

ADDITIONAL LYRICS

2. LET ME TELL YOU, BABE, WHAT I SAY IS TRUE.
   I AIN'T NEVER, NEVER LOVED NOBODY IN THE WAY THAT I LOVE YOU, NO,
   YOU GOT ME DIZZY,
   WHOA, YOU GOT ME DIZZY.
   YEAH, YOU GOT ME DIZZY
   AND I CAN'T EVEN SEE MY WAY.

3. WAIT A MINUTE, BABE, DON'T YOU BIP OR BOP.
   YOU DONE MADE ME LOVE YOU, BABY, AND I SWEAR I JUST CAN'T STOP,
   'CAUSE YOU GOT ME DIZZY,
   WHOA, YOU GOT ME DIZZY.
   YEAH, YOU GOT ME DIZZY
   AND I CAN'T EVEN SEE MY WAY.

Ain't That Lovin' You Baby

Words and Music by
Jimmy Reed

Additional Lyrics

2. Let me tell you, baby,
   Don't sound like it's true.
   They could drop me in the ocean,
   I'd swim to the bank and
   Crawl home to you.

3. They may kill me, baby,
   Bury me just like they do.
   My body might lie,
   But my spirit gonna rise and
   Come home to you.

CD TRACK

2 FULL STEREO MIX

10 SPLIT MIX

C VERSION

Baby, What You Want Me to Do

Words and Music by
Jimmy Reed

BA - BY, WHY YOU WAN - NA LET GO? _____

2. GO - IN'

HARP SOLO

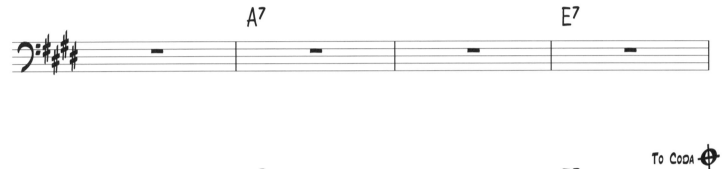

To Coda

D.S. AL CODA
(TAKE 2ND ENDING)

CODA

3. YOU GOT ME

(GUITAR)

ADDITIONAL LYRICS

2. GOIN' UP, GOIN' DOWN,
   GOIN' UP, DOWN, DOWN, UP ANY WAY YOU WANNA, LET IT ROLL.
   YEAH, YEAH, YEAH.
   YOU GOT ME DOIN' WHAT YOU WANT ME,
   BABY, WHY YOU WANNA LET GO?

3. YOU GOT ME PEEPIN', YOU GOT ME HIDIN',
   YOU GOT ME PEEP, HIDE, HIDE, PEEP ANY WAY YOU WANNA, LET IT ROLL.
   YEAH, YEAH, YEAH.
   YOU GOT ME DOIN' WHAT YOU WANT ME,
   BABY, WHY YOU WANNA LET GO?

Big Boss Man

Words and Music by
Al Smith and Luther Dixon

Additional Lyrics

2. Well, I'm gonna get me a boss man,
   One gonna treat me right.
   Work hard in the daytime,
   Rest easy at night.
   Big boss man,
   Can't you hear me when I call?
   Well, you ain't so big,
   You just tall, that's all.

Bright Lights, Big City

Words and Music by
Jimmy Reed

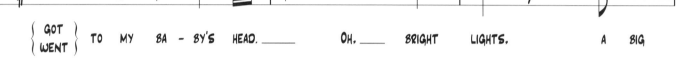

NEED MY HELP SOME-DAY. ___ OH, ___ YES AL - RIGHT, A PRET-TY

BA - BY, ___ YOU'RE GON - NA NEED MY HELP ___ SOME-DAY. ___ YOU'RE GON - NA

WISH YOU HAD A LIS-TENED TO SOME OF THOSE THINGS I SAID. ___

SOLO

3. A GO ___

VERSE

'HEAD _____ PRET-TY BA - BY, ___ A HON-EY, KNOCK A YOUR - SELF OUT. ___

___ OH, ___ GO 'HEAD A PRET - TY BA - BY, ___ A

HON - EY, KNOCK ___ YOUR - SELF OUT. ___ I ___ STILL ___ LOVE YOU BA - BY 'CAUSE YOU

D.S. AL FINE

DON'T KNOW WHAT IT'S ALL A - BOUT. ___ 4. BRIGHT

Additional Lyrics

2. I've been down south, you know, I've been out east.
I've been out west, but I'm not gonna rest 'til I
Get to New York, I'm goin' to New York.
I'm goin' to New York, I'm goin' if I have to walk.

3. I've been here, you know, I've been there.
Honey, I've been some of everywhere, but I'm
Goin' to New York, I'm goin' to New York.
I'm goin' to New York, I'm goin' if I have to walk.

Honest I Do

Words and Music by
Jimmy Reed and Ewart G. Abner, Jr.

INTRO-SOLO
SLOW SHUFFLE ♩ = 66

(HARP)

1. Don't you know that I love _____ you.
2. See additional lyrics

HON - EST I DO. _____

I'D NEV - ER PLACE _____

NO ONE _____ A - BOVE YOU.

To Coda

BRIDGE

D7

Please tell me you love _____ me.

E7

Stop driv - in' me mad. _____

You the sweet - est lit - tle wom - an

D.S. al Coda

A

that I ev - er had. _____

Coda **OUTRO-SOLO**

A

(Harp)

E7

A

Repeat and Fade

ADDITIONAL LYRICS

2. I told you I love you,
   Stop drivin' me mad.
   When I woke up this morning,
   I never felt so bad.

You Don't Have to Go

Words and Music by
Jimmy Reed

YEAH,   YOU   GOT   ME   DIZ - ZY,   AND   I
CAN'T   E - VEN   SEE   MY   WAY. _____

HARP SOLOS

Additional Lyrics

2. Let me tell you, babe, what I say is true.
   I ain't never, never loved nobody in the way that I love you, no,
   You got me dizzy,
   Whoa, you got me dizzy.
   Yeah, you got me dizzy
   And I can't even see my way.

3. Wait a minute, babe, don't you bip or bop.
   You done made me love you, baby, and I swear I just can't stop,
   'Cause you got me dizzy,
   Whoa, you got me dizzy.
   Yeah, you got me dizzy
   And I can't even see my way.

Presenting the Hal Leonard JAZZ PLAY-ALONG SERIES

For use with all B-flat, E-flat, Bass Clef and C instruments, the Jazz Play-Along® Series is the ultimate learning tool for all jazz musicians. With musician-friendly lead sheets, melody cues, and other split-track choices on the included CD, these first-of-a-kind packages help you master improvisation while playing some of the greatest tunes of all time. FOR STUDY, each tune includes a split track with: melody cue with proper style and inflection • professional rhythm tracks • choruses for soloing • removable bass part • removable piano part. FOR PERFORMANCE, each tune also has: an additional full stereo accompaniment track (no melody) • additional choruses for soloing.

1. DUKE ELLINGTON
   00841644..........................$16.95

1A. MAIDEN VOYAGE/ALL BLUES
   00843158 ....$15.99

2. MILES DAVIS
   00841645..........................$16.95

3. THE BLUES
   00841646..........................$16.99

4. JAZZ BALLADS
   00841691..........................$16.99

5. BEST OF BEBOP
   00841689..........................$16.95

6. JAZZ CLASSICS WITH EASY CHANGES
   00841690..........................$16.99

7. ESSENTIAL JAZZ STANDARDS
   00843000..........................$16.99

8. ANTONIO CARLOS JOBIM AND THE ART OF THE BOSSA NOVA
   00843001..........................$16.95

9. DIZZY GILLESPIE
   00843002..........................$16.99

10. DISNEY CLASSICS
   00843003..........................$16.99

11. RODGERS AND HART FAVORITES
   00843004..........................$16.99

12. ESSENTIAL JAZZ CLASSICS
   00843005..........................$16.99

13. JOHN COLTRANE
   00843006..........................$16.95

14. IRVING BERLIN
   00843007..........................$15.99

15. RODGERS & HAMMERSTEIN
   00843008..........................$15.99

16. COLE PORTER
   00843009..........................$15.95

17. COUNT BASIE
   00843010..........................$16.95

18. HAROLD ARLEN
   00843011..........................$15.95

19. COOL JAZZ
   00843012..........................$15.95

20. CHRISTMAS CAROLS
   00843080..........................$14.95

21. RODGERS AND HART CLASSICS
   00843014..........................$14.95

22. WAYNE SHORTER
   00843015..........................$16.95

23. LATIN JAZZ
   00843016..........................$16.95

24. EARLY JAZZ STANDARDS
   00843017..........................$14.95

25. CHRISTMAS JAZZ
   00843018..........................$16.95

26. CHARLIE PARKER
   00843019..........................$16.95

27. GREAT JAZZ STANDARDS
   00843020..........................$16.99

28. BIG BAND ERA
   00843021..........................$15.99

29. LENNON AND MCCARTNEY
   00843022..........................$16.95

30. BLUES' BEST
   00843023..........................$15.99

31. JAZZ IN THREE
   00843024..........................$15.99

32. BEST OF SWING
   00843025..........................$15.99

33. SONNY ROLLINS
   00843029..........................$15.95

34. ALL TIME STANDARDS
   00843030..........................$15.99

35. BLUESY JAZZ
   00843031..........................$16.99

36. HORACE SILVER
   00843032..........................$16.99

37. BILL EVANS
   00843033..........................$16.95

38. YULETIDE JAZZ
   00843034..........................$16.95

39. "ALL THE THINGS YOU ARE" & MORE JEROME KERN SONGS
   00843035..........................$15.99

40. BOSSA NOVA
   00843036..........................$15.99

41. CLASSIC DUKE ELLINGTON
   00843037..........................$16.99

42. GERRY MULLIGAN FAVORITES
   00843038..........................$16.99

43. GERRY MULLIGAN CLASSICS
   00843039..........................$16.95

44. OLIVER NELSON
   00843040..........................$16.95

45. JAZZ AT THE MOVIES
   00843041..........................$15.99

46. BROADWAY JAZZ STANDARDS
   00843042..........................$15.99

47. CLASSIC JAZZ BALLADS
   00843043..........................$15.99

48. BEBOP CLASSICS
   00843044..........................$16.99

49. MILES DAVIS STANDARDS
   00843045..........................$16.95

50. GREAT JAZZ CLASSICS
   00843046..........................$15.99

51. UP-TEMPO JAZZ
   00843047..........................$15.99

52. STEVIE WONDER
   00843048..........................$16.99

53. RHYTHM CHANGES
   00843049..........................$15.99

54. "MOONLIGHT IN VERMONT" AND OTHER GREAT STANDARDS
   00843050..........................$15.99

55. BENNY GOLSON
   00843052..........................$15.95

56. "GEORGIA ON MY MIND" & OTHER SONGS BY HOAGY CARMICHAEL
   00843056 ....$15.99

57. VINCE GUARALDI
   00843057..........................$16.99

58. MORE LENNON AND MCCARTNEY
   00843059..........................$15.99

59. SOUL JAZZ 00843060...............$15.99	**86. BENNY GOODMAN** 00843110...............$14.95	**113. PAQUITO D'RIVERA – BRAZILIAN JAZZ** 48020663...............$19.99
60. DEXTER GORDON 00843061...............$15.95	**87. DIXIELAND** 00843111...............$14.95	**114. MODERN JAZZ QUARTET FAVORITES** 00843163...............$15.99
61. MONGO SANTAMARIA 00843062...............$15.95	**88. DUKE ELLINGTON FAVORITES** 00843112...............$14.95	**115. THE SOUND OF MUSIC** 00843164...............$15.99
62. JAZZ-ROCK FUSION 00843063...............$16.99	**89. IRVING BERLIN FAVORITES** 00843113...............$14.95	**116. JACO PASTORIUS** 00843165...............$15.99
63. CLASSICAL JAZZ 00843064...............$14.95	**90. THELONIOUS MONK CLASSICS** 00841262...............$16.99	**117. ANTONIO CARLOS JOBIM – MORE HITS** 00843166...............$15.99
64. TV TUNES 00843065...............$14.95	**91. THELONIOUS MONK FAVORITES** 00841263...............$16.99	**118. BIG JAZZ STANDARDS COLLECTION** 00843167...............$27.50
65. SMOOTH JAZZ 00843066...............$16.99	**92. LEONARD BERNSTEIN** 00450134...............$15.99	**119. JELLY ROLL MORTON** 00843168...............$15.99
66. A CHARLIE BROWN CHRISTMAS 00843067...............$16.99	**93. DISNEY FAVORITES** 00843142...............$14.99	**120. J.S. BACH** 00843169...............$15.99
67. CHICK COREA 00843068...............$15.95	**94. RAY** 00843143...............$14.99	**121. DJANGO REINHARDT** 00843170...............$15.99
68. CHARLES MINGUS 00843069...............$16.95	**95. JAZZ AT THE LOUNGE** 00843144...............$14.99	**122. PAUL SIMON** 00843182...............$16.99
69. CLASSIC JAZZ 00843071...............$15.99	**96. LATIN JAZZ STANDARDS** 00843145...............$14.99	**123. BACHARACH & DAVID** 00843185...............$15.99
70. THE DOORS 00843072...............$14.95	**97. MAYBE I'M AMAZED** 00843148...............$15.99	**124. JAZZ-ROCK HORN HITS** 00843186...............$15.99
71. COLE PORTER CLASSICS 00843073...............$14.95	**98. DAVE FRISHBERG** 00843149...............$15.99	**126. COUNT BASIE CLASSICS** 00843157...............$15.99
72. CLASSIC JAZZ BALLADS 00843074...............$15.99	**99. SWINGING STANDARDS** 00843150...............$14.99	**127. CHUCK MANGIONE** 00843188...............$15.99
73. JAZZ/BLUES 00843075...............$14.95	**100. LOUIS ARMSTRONG** 00740423...............$15.99	**132. STAN GETZ ESSENTIALS** 00843193...............$15.99
74. BEST JAZZ CLASSICS 00843076...............$15.99	**101. BUD POWELL** 00843152...............$14.99	**133. STAN GETZ FAVORITES** 00843194...............$15.99
75. PAUL DESMOND 00843077...............$14.95	**102. JAZZ POP** 00843153...............$14.99	**135. JEFF BECK** 00843197...............$15.99
76. BROADWAY JAZZ BALLADS 00843078...............$15.99	**103. ON GREEN DOLPHIN STREET & OTHER JAZZ CLASSICS** 00843154...............$14.99	**137. WES MONTGOMERY** 00843199...............$15.99
77. JAZZ ON BROADWAY 00843079...............$15.99	**104. ELTON JOHN** 00843155...............$14.99	**139. JULIAN "CANNONBALL" ADDERLEY** 00843201...............$15.99
78. STEELY DAN 00843070...............$14.99	**105. SOULFUL JAZZ** 00843151...............$15.99	**150. JAZZ IMPROV BASICS** 00843195...............$19.99
79. MILES DAVIS CLASSICS 00843081...............$15.99	**106. SLO' JAZZ** 00843117...............$14.99	
80. JIMI HENDRIX 00843083...............$15.99	**107. MOTOWN CLASSICS** 00843116...............$14.99	
81. FRANK SINATRA – CLASSICS 00843084...............$15.99	**108. JAZZ WALTZ** 00843159...............$15.99	
82. FRANK SINATRA – STANDARDS 00843085...............$15.99	**109. OSCAR PETERSON** 00843160...............$16.99	
83. ANDREW LLOYD WEBBER 00843104...............$14.95	**110. JUST STANDARDS** 00843161...............$15.99	
84. BOSSA NOVA CLASSICS 00843105...............$14.95	**111. COOL CHRISTMAS** 00843162...............$15.99	
85. MOTOWN HITS 00843109...............$14.95	**112. PAQUITO D'RIVERA – LATIN JAZZ** 48020662...............$16.99	

Prices, contents, and availability subject to change without notice.

FOR MORE INFORMATION,
SEE YOUR LOCAL MUSIC DEALER,
OR WRITE TO:

HAL•LEONARD®
CORPORATION
7777 W. BLUEMOUND RD. P.O. BOX 13819
MILWAUKEE, WISCONSIN 53213
For complete songlists and more,
visit Hal Leonard online at

www.halleonard.com

0311

HAL•LEONARD

BLUES PLAY-ALONG

For use with all the C, B♭, Bass Clef and E♭ Instruments, the Hal Leonard Blues Play-Along Series is the ultimate jamming tool for all blues musicians.

With easy-to-read lead sheets, and other split-track choices on the included CD, these first-of-a-kind packages will bring your local blues jam right into your house! Each song on the CD includes two tracks: a full stereo mix, and a split track mix with removable guitar, bass, piano, and harp parts. The CD is playable on any CD player, and is also enhanced so Mac and PC users can adjust the recording to any tempo without changing the pitch!

1. Chicago Blues
All Your Love (I Miss Loving) • Easy Baby • I Ain't Got You • I'm Your Hoochie Coochie Man • Killing Floor • Mary Had a Little Lamb • Messin' with the Kid • Sweet Home Chicago.

00843106 Book/CD Pack $12.99

2. Texas Blues
Hide Away • If You Love Me Like You Say • Mojo Hand • Okie Dokie Stomp • Pride and Joy • Reconsider Baby • T-Bone Shuffle • The Things That I Used to Do.

00843107 Book/CD Pack $12.99

3. Slow Blues
Don't Throw Your Love on Me So Strong • Five Long Years • I Can't Quit You Baby • I Just Want to Make Love to You • The Sky Is Crying • (They Call It) Stormy Monday (Stormy Monday Blues) • Sweet Little Angel • Texas Flood.

00843108 Book/CD Pack $12.99

4. Shuffle Blues
Beautician Blues • Bright Lights, Big City • Further on up the Road • I'm Tore Down • Juke • Let Me Love You Baby • Look at Little Sister • Rock Me Baby.

00843171 Book/CD Pack $12.99

5. B.B. King
Everyday I Have the Blues • It's My Own Fault Darlin' • Just Like a Woman • Please Accept My Love • Sweet Sixteen • The Thrill Is Gone • Why I Sing the Blues • You Upset Me Baby.

00843172 Book/CD Pack $14.99

6. Jazz Blues
Birk's Works • Blues in the Closet • Cousin Mary • Freddie Freeloader • Now's the Time • Tenor Madness • Things Ain't What They Used to Be • Turnaround.

00843175 Book/CD Pack $12.99

7. Howlin' Wolf
Built for Comfort • Forty-Four • How Many More Years • Killing Floor • Moanin' at Midnight • Shake for Me • Sitting on Top of the World • Smokestack Lightning.

00843176 Book/CD Pack $12.99

8. Blues Classics
Baby, Please Don't Go • Boom Boom • Born Under a Bad Sign • Dust My Broom • How Long, How Long Blues • I Ain't Superstitious • It Hurts Me Too • My Babe.

00843177 Book/CD Pack $12.99

9. Albert Collins
Brick • Collins' Mix • Don't Lose Your Cool • Frost Bite • Frosty • I Ain't Drunk • Master Charge • Trash Talkin'.

00843178 Book/CD Pack $12.99

10. Uptempo Blues
Cross Road Blues (Crossroads) • Give Me Back My Wig • Got My Mo Jo Working • The House Is Rockin' • Paying the Cost to Be the Boss • Rollin' and Tumblin' • Turn on Your Love Light • You Can't Judge a Book by the Cover.

00843179 Book/CD Pack $12.99

11. Christmas Blues
Back Door Santa • Blue Christmas • Dig That Crazy Santa Claus • Merry Christmas, Baby • Please Come Home for Christmas • Santa Baby • Soulful Christmas.

00843203 Book/CD Pack $12.99

FOR MORE INFORMATION, SEE YOUR LOCAL MUSIC DEALER, OR WRITE TO:

HAL•LEONARD® CORPORATION
7777 W. BLUEMOUND RD. P.O. BOX 13819 MILWAUKEE, WI 53213

www.halleonard.com

Prices, content, and availability subject to change without notice.

The Best-Selling Jazz Book of All Time Is Now Legal!

The Real Books are the most popular jazz books of all time. Since the 1970s, musicians have trusted these volumes to get them through every gig, night after night. The problem is that the books were illegally produced and distributed, without any regard to copyright law, or royalties paid to the composers who created these musical masterpieces.

Hal Leonard is very proud to present the first legitimate and legal editions of these books ever produced. You won't even notice the difference, other than all the notorious errors being fixed: the covers and typeface look the same, the song lists are nearly identical, and the price for our edition is even cheaper than the originals!

Every conscientious musician will appreciate that these books are now produced accurately and ethically, benefitting the songwriters that we owe for some of the greatest tunes of all time!

VOLUME 1
Includes: Autumn Leaves • Body and Soul • Don't Get Around Much Anymore • Falling in Love with Love • Have You Met Miss Jones? • Lullaby of Birdland • Misty • Satin Doll • Stella by Starlight • and hundreds more!

00240221	C Edition	$29.99
00240224	B♭ Edition	$29.95
00240225	E♭ Edition	$29.99
00240226	Bass Clef Edition	$29.95
00240292	C Edition 6 x 9	$27.95
00451087	C Edition on CD-ROM	$25.00

VOLUME 2
Includes: Avalon • Birdland • Come Rain or Come Shine • Fever • Georgia on My Mind • It Might as Well Be Spring • Moonglow • The Nearness of You • On the Sunny Side of the Street • Route 66 • Sentimental Journey • Smoke Gets in Your Eyes • Tangerine • Yardbird Suite • and more!

00240222	C Edition	$29.99
00240227	B♭ Edition	$29.95
00240228	E♭ Edition	$29.95
00240229	Bass Clef Edition	$29.95
00240293	C Edition 6 x 9	$27.95

VOLUME 3
Includes: Ain't Misbehavin' • Cheek to Cheek • The Lady Is a Tramp • A Nightingale Sang in Berkeley Square • On a Clear Day • Stormy Weather • The Very Thought of You • and more!

00240233	C Edition	$29.99
00240284	B♭ Edition	$29.95
00240285	E♭ Edition	$29.95
00240286	Bass Clef Edition	$29.95

VOLUME 4
Includes: The Best Is Yet to Come • A Foggy Day (In London Town) • I Got Rhythm • Kansas City • Night and Day • Ol' Man River • Smile • Them There Eyes • and more!

00240296	C Edition	$29.99

Play-along CDs to some of the most popular songs featured in the world famous *Real Books* are available. Each volume features selections sorted alphabetically from the 6th edition, each in 3-CD sets.

The Real Book Play-Along – Volume 1
00240302	A-D	$24.99
00240303	E-J	$24.95
00240304	L-R	$24.95
00240305	S-Z	$24.99

The Real Book Play-Along – Volume 2
00240351	A-D	$24.99
00240352	E-I	$24.99
00240353	J-R	$24.99
00240354	S-Z	$24.99

Also available:
00240264	The Real Blues Book	$34.99
00240306	The Real Christmas Book	$25.00
00240137	Miles Davis Real Book	$19.95
00240235	The Duke Ellington Real Book	$19.99
00240331	The Bud Powell Real Book	$19.99
00240313	The Real Rock Book	$29.99
00240359	The Real Tab Book – Vol. 1	$32.50
00310910	The Real Bluegrass Book	$29.99
00240355	The Real Dixieland Book	$29.99
00240317	The Real Worship Book	$29.99

THE REAL VOCAL BOOK
00240230	Volume 1 High Voice	$29.95
00240307	Volume 1 Low Voice	$29.99
00240231	Volume 2 High Voice	$29.95
00240308	Volume 2 Low Voice	$29.95

THE REAL BOOK – STAFF PAPER
00240327	$9.95

FOR MORE INFORMATION, SEE YOUR LOCAL MUSIC DEALER,
OR WRITE TO:

HAL•LEONARD® CORPORATION
7777 W. BLUEMOUND RD. P.O. BOX 13819 MILWAUKEE, WI 53213

Complete song lists online at www.halleonard.com
Prices and availability subject to change without notice.

0111

Jazz Instruction & Improvisation
Books for All Instruments from Hal Leonard

AN APPROACH TO JAZZ IMPROVISATION
by Dave Pozzi
Musicians Institute Press
Explore the styles of Charlie Parker, Sonny Rollins, Bud Powell and others with this comprehensive guide to jazz improvisation. Covers: scale choices • chord analysis • phrasing • melodies • harmonic progressions • more.
00695135 Book/CD Pack $17.95

INCLUDES TAB

BUILDING A JAZZ VOCABULARY
By Mike Steinel
A valuable resource for learning the basics of jazz from Mike Steinel of the University of North Texas. It covers: the basics of jazz • how to build effective solos • a comprehensive practice routine • and a jazz vocabulary of the masters.
00849911 ....$19.95

THE CYCLE OF FIFTHS
by Emile and Laura De Cosmo
This essential instruction book provides more than 450 exercises, including hundreds of melodic and rhythmic ideas. The book is designed to help improvisors master the cycle of fifths, one of the primary progressions in music. Guaranteed to refine technique, enhance improvisational fluency, and improve sight-reading!
00311114 ....$16.99

THE DIATONIC CYCLE
by Emile and Laura De Cosmo
Renowned jazz educators Emile and Laura De Cosmo provide more than 300 exercises to help improvisors tackle one of music's most common progressions: the diatonic cycle. This book is guaranteed to refine technique, enhance improvisational fluency, and improve sight-reading!
00311115 ....$16.95

EAR TRAINING
by Keith Wyatt,
Carl Schroeder and Joe Elliott
Musicians Institute Press
Covers: basic pitch matching • singing major and minor scales • identifying intervals • transcribing melodies and rhythm • identifying chords and progressions • seventh chords and the blues • modal interchange, chromaticism, modulation • and more.
00695198 Book/2-CD Pack...................$24.95

EXERCISES AND ETUDES FOR THE JAZZ INSTRUMENTALIST
by J.J. Johnson
Designed as study material and playable by any instrument, these pieces run the gamut of the jazz experience, featuring common and uncommon time signatures and keys, and styles from ballads to funk. They are progressively graded so that both beginners and professionals will be challenged by the demands of this wonderful music.
00842018 Bass Clef Edition...................$16.95
00842042 Treble Clef Edition $16.95

JAZZOLOGY
THE ENCYCLOPEDIA OF JAZZ THEORY FOR ALL MUSICIANS
by Robert Rawlins and Nor Eddine Bahha
This comprehensive resource covers a variety of jazz topics, for beginners and pros of any instrument. The book serves as an encyclopedia for reference, a thorough methodology for the student, and a workbook for the classroom.
00311167 ....$18.95

JAZZ JAM SESSION
15 TRACKS INCLUDING RHYTHM CHANGES, BLUES, BOSSA, BALLADS & MORE
by Ed Friedland
Bring your local jazz jam session home! These essential jazz rhythm grooves feature a professional rhythm section and are perfect for guitar, harmonica, keyboard, saxophone and trumpet players to hone their soloing skills. The feels, tempos and keys have been varied to broaden your jazz experience. Styles include: ballads, bebop, blues, bossa nova, cool jazz, and more, with improv guidelines for each track.
_____00311827 Book/CD Pack $19.99

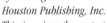

JAZZ THEORY RESOURCES
by Bert Ligon
Houston Publishing, Inc.
This is a jazz theory text in two volumes. **Volume 1 includes:** review of basic theory • rhythm in jazz performance • triadic generalization • diatonic harmonic progressions and analysis • substitutions and turnarounds • and more. **Volume 2 includes:** modes and modal frameworks • quartal harmony • extended tertian structures and triadic superimposition • pentatonic applications • coloring "outside" the lines and beyond • and more.
00030458 Volume 1 ....$39.95
00030459 Volume 2 ....$29.95

Prices, contents & availability subject to change without notice.

JOY OF IMPROV
by Dave Frank and John Amaral
This book/CD course on improvisation for all instruments and all styles will help players develop monster musical skills! **Book One** imparts a solid basis in technique, rhythm, chord theory, ear training and improv concepts. **Book Two** explores more advanced chord voicings, chord arranging techniques and more challenging blues and melodic lines. The CD can be used as a listening and play-along tool.
00220005 Book 1 – Book/CD Pack $27.99
00220006 Book 2 – Book/CD Pack $24.95

THE PATH TO JAZZ IMPROVISATION
by Emile and Laura De Cosmo
This fascinating jazz instruction book offers an innovative, scholarly approach to the art of improvisation. It includes in-depth analysis and lessons about: cycle of fifths • diatonic cycle • overtone series • pentatonic scale • harmonic and melodic minor scale • polytonal order of keys • blues and bebop scales • modes • and more.
00310904 ....$14.95

THE SOURCE
THE DICTIONARY OF CONTEMPORARY AND TRADITIONAL SCALES
by Steve Barta
This book serves as an informative guide for people who are looking for good, solid information regarding scales, chords, and how they work together. It provides right and left hand fingerings for scales, chords, and complete inversions. Includes over 20 different scales, each written in all 12 keys.
00240885 ....$15.95

21 BEBOP EXERCISES
by Steve Rawlins
This book/CD pack is both a warm-up collection and a manual for bebop phrasing. Its tasty and sophisticated exercises will help you develop your proficiency with jazz interpretation. It concentrates on practice in all twelve keys – moving higher by half-step – to help develop dexterity and range. The companion CD includes all of the exercises in 12 keys.
00315341 Book/CD Pack $17.95